Super Bob and the Birthday Surprise

written and illustrated by
Matthew Urmenyhazi

Rigby • Saxon • Steck-Vaughn

www.HarcourtAchieve.com
1.800.531.5015

Characters

Super Bob

Otto

Tammy

Contents

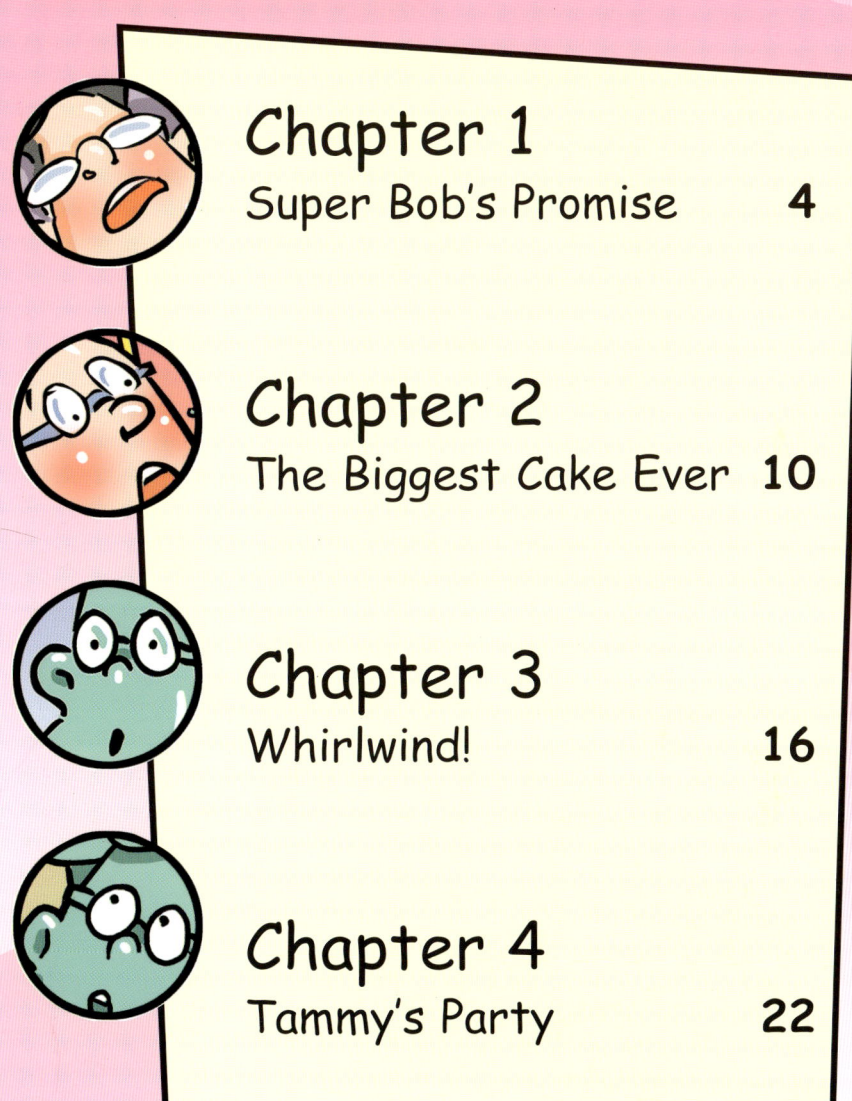

Chapter 1
Super Bob's Promise 4

Chapter 2
The Biggest Cake Ever 10

Chapter 3
Whirlwind! 16

Chapter 4
Tammy's Party 22

Chapter 1

Super Bob's Promise

Super Bob and Otto were at the beach. Super Bob threw the ball across the water.

"Catch the ball, Otto!" he yelled. The ball bounced off Otto's head with a thud. It was a great day for fun in the sun.

Otto felt dizzy. He laid down for a nap. "A quick nap is a good idea!" Super Bob said to his trusty plastic pal.

Otto laid on the sand. Bob rested his head on Otto's tummy.

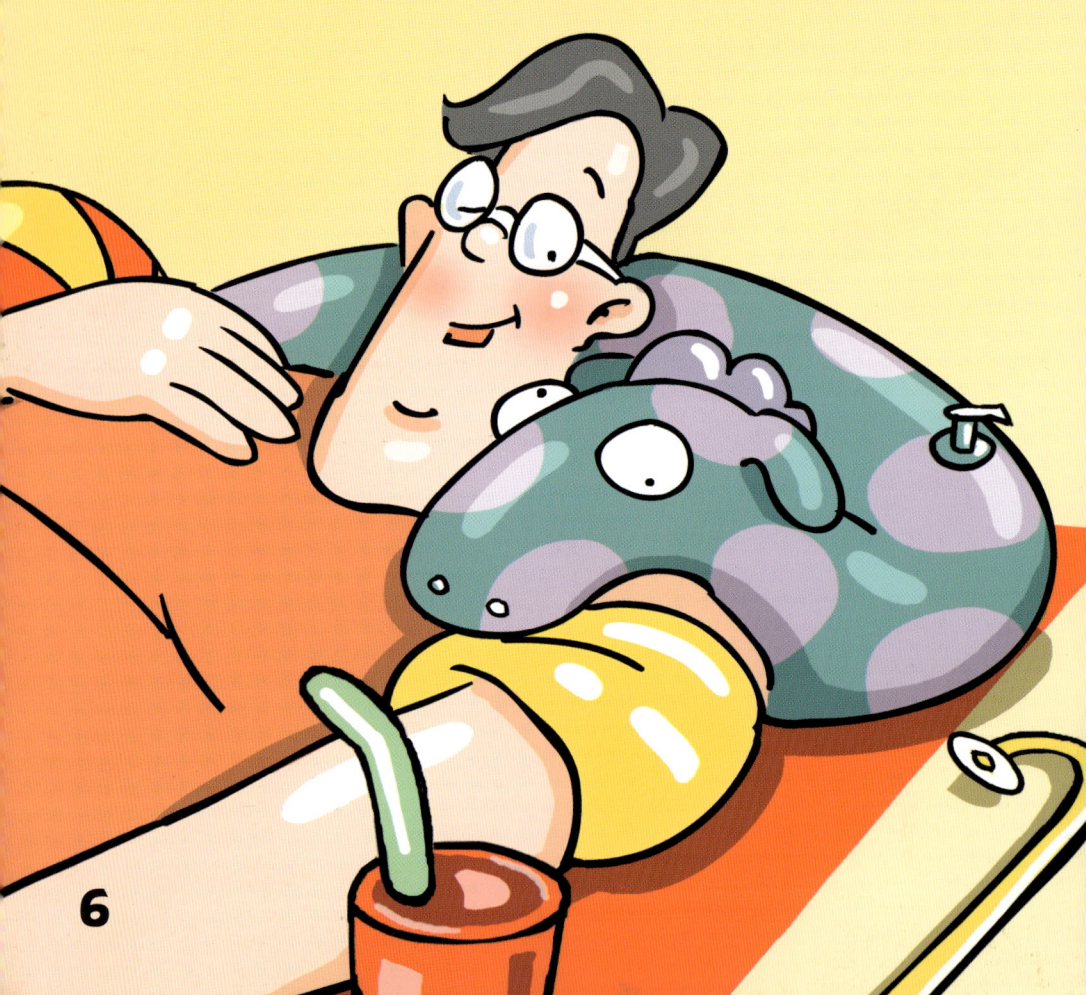

Super Bob fell fast asleep. He dreamed about his favorite things. He dreamed about sweets and ice creams, drinks and cakes.

"Mmmm, cake!" mumbled Super Bob, sitting up with a jolt. He had promised to make a cake for Tammy's birthday. And her birthday party was today.

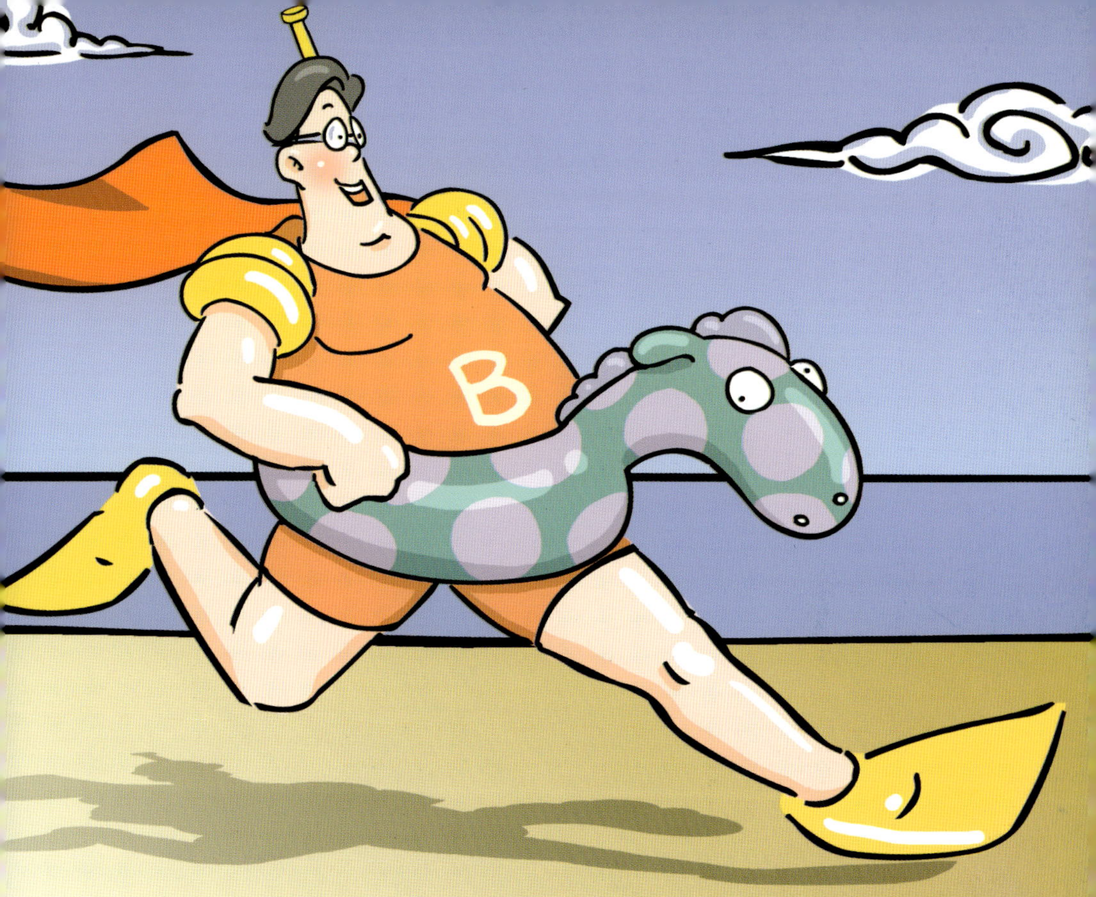

"We'd better get going, Otto. We have a cake to bake!"

Super Bob bounded toward the stores. Otto nodded, his head bouncing up and down with each footstep.

Chapter 2

The Biggest Cake Ever

Super Bob liked shopping. He filled the cart with sugar and flour, chocolate and icing, eggs and butter.

"We will make Tammy the biggest birthday cake she has ever seen," said Super Bob.

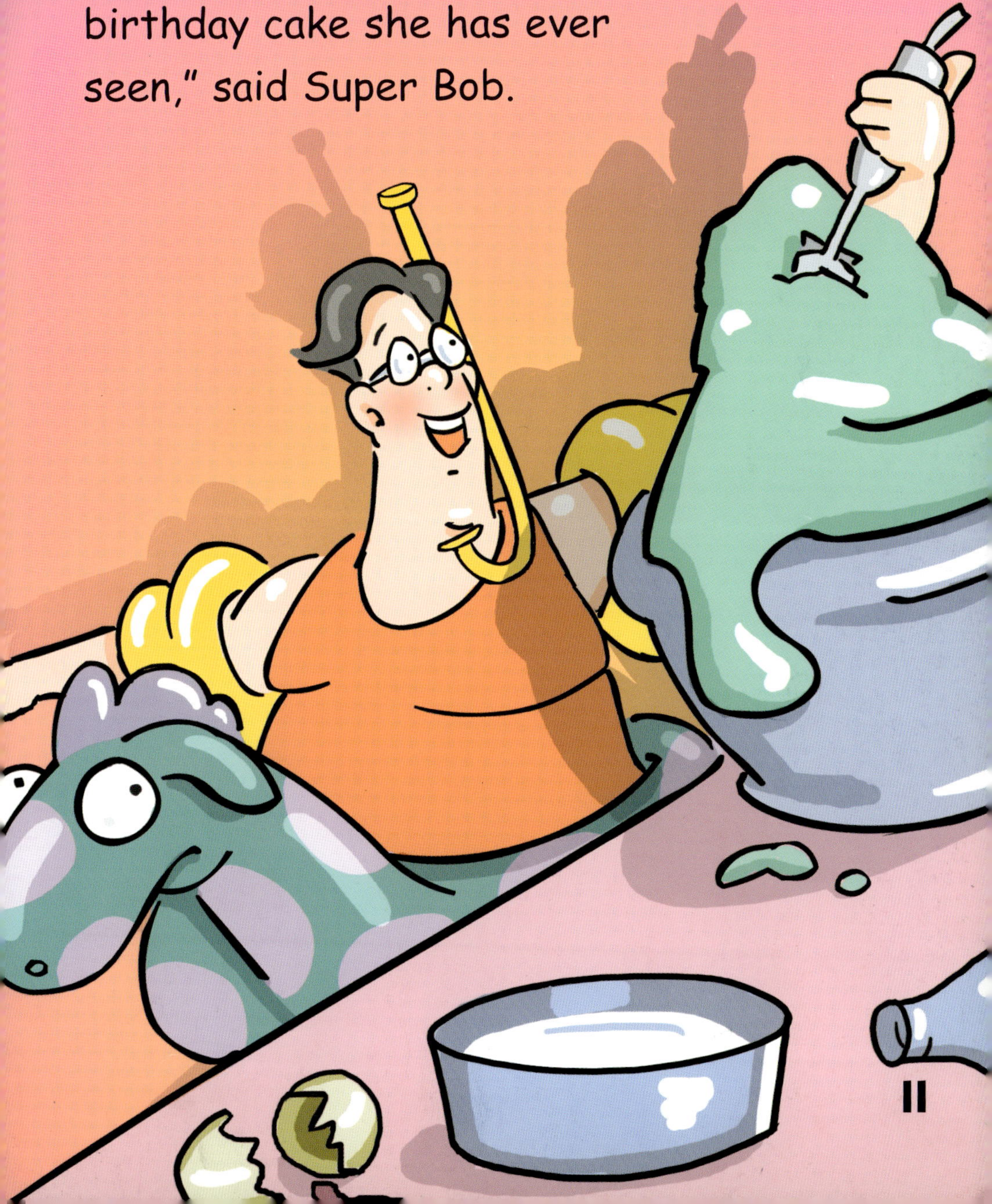

"Now I think that's everything. Stand back, Otto. Things could get messy."

Super Bob flicked the switch.

"Uh-oh . . . the mixer is too fast! I don't think I can hold it!"

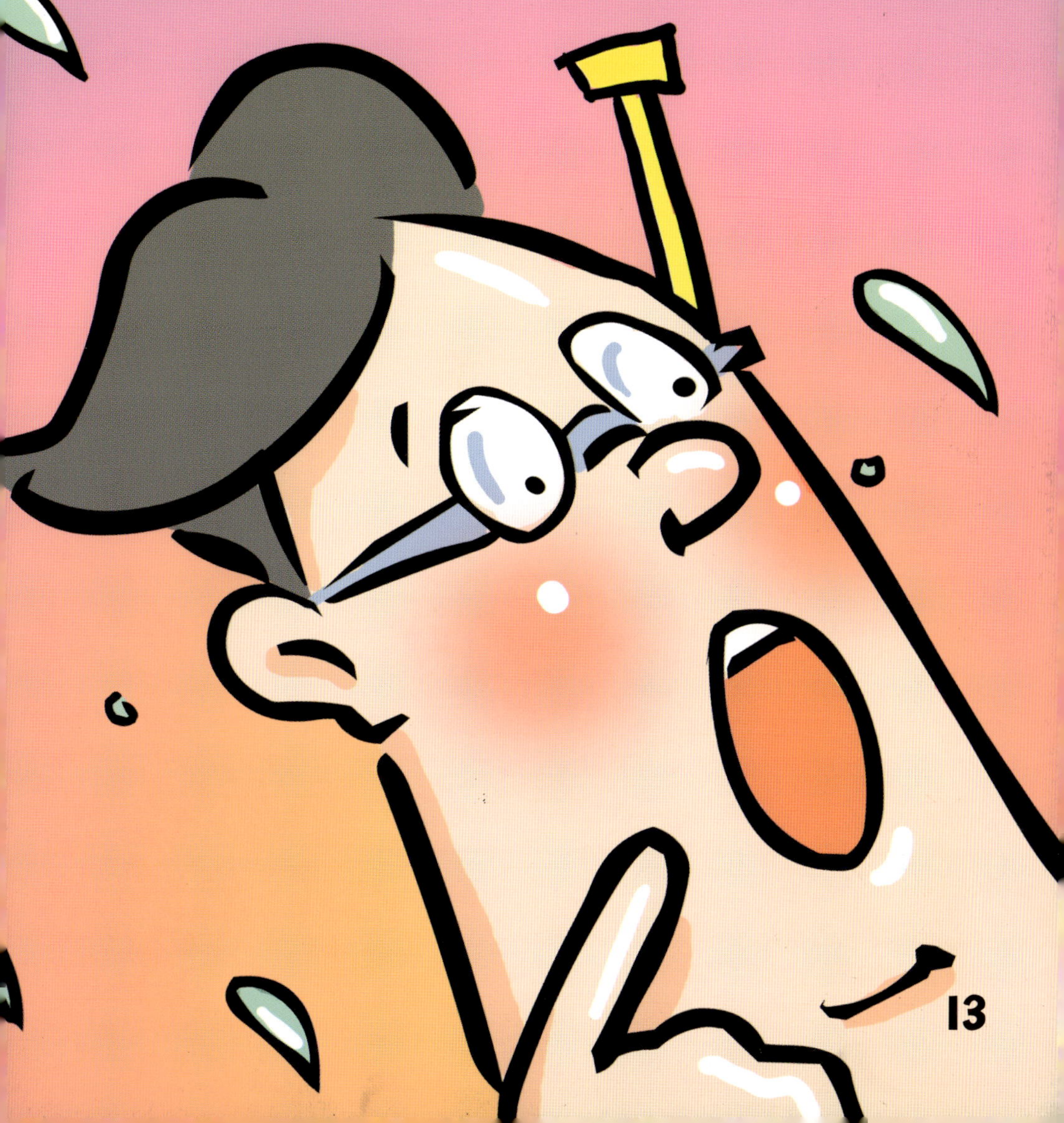

"Ooops! It's quick-drying cake mix," Super Bob said as he licked his lips.

"Mmmm . . . Yum! At least it tastes good. Never mind, little buddy. It's party time! Tammy's party is about to start."

Chapter 3

Whirlwind!

Super Bob ran down the street. Otto bounced along with him.

"Uh-oh . . . looks like there could be a storm ahead!" said Super Bob.

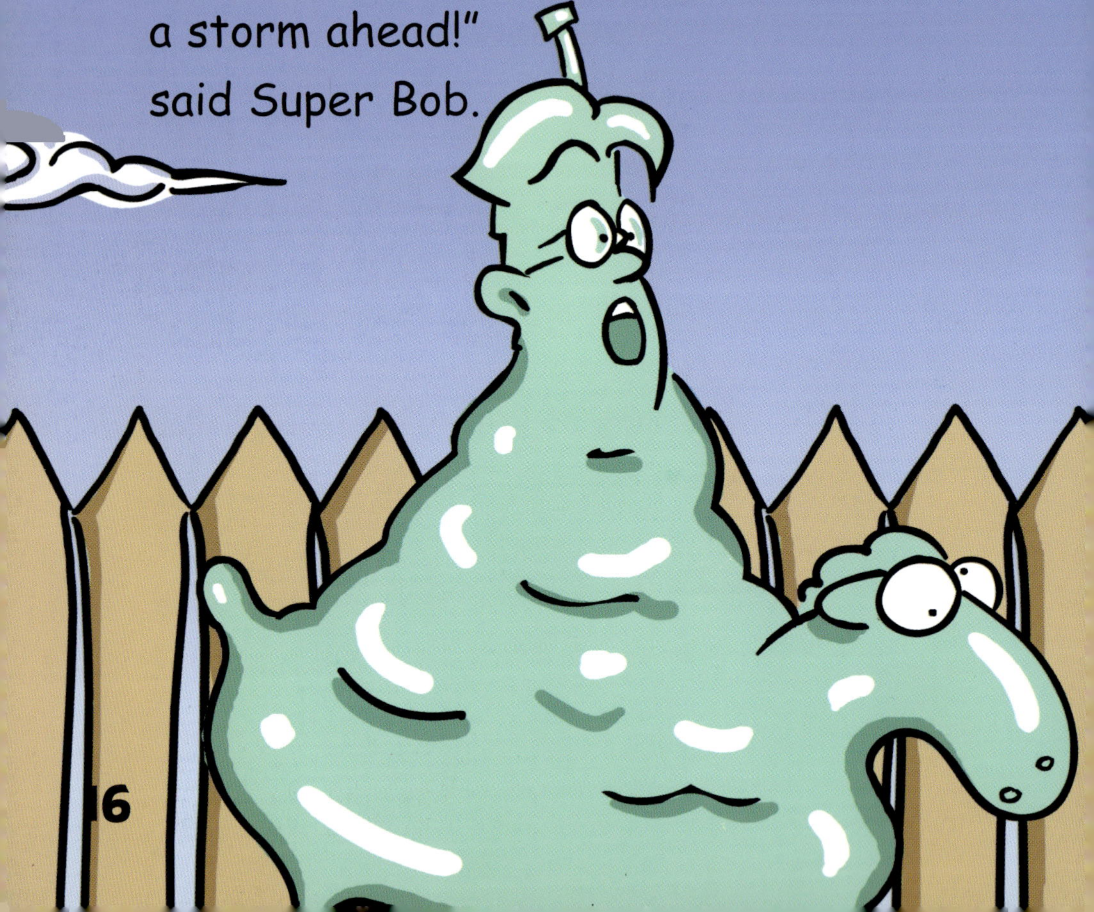

The storm clouds rolled in.
The wind got stronger.

The wind blew down onto the street.
It picked up piles of leaves from
the gutter.

Super Bob was in the middle of a colorful whirlwind.

"Oh, no," said Super Bob, as the leaves stuck to him. "I look like a tree. Stay with me, Otto."

Now Super Bob was in a real hurry. He didn't want to be late for Tammy's party.

He waved to his friend, Jim. Jim was painting his fence with thick red paint.

Super Bob stepped into a pot of red paint. "Uh-oh, I am clumsy today."

"Oh, no! I'm a tree in a pot. I do hope no one tries to water me!"

Chapter 4

Tammy's Party

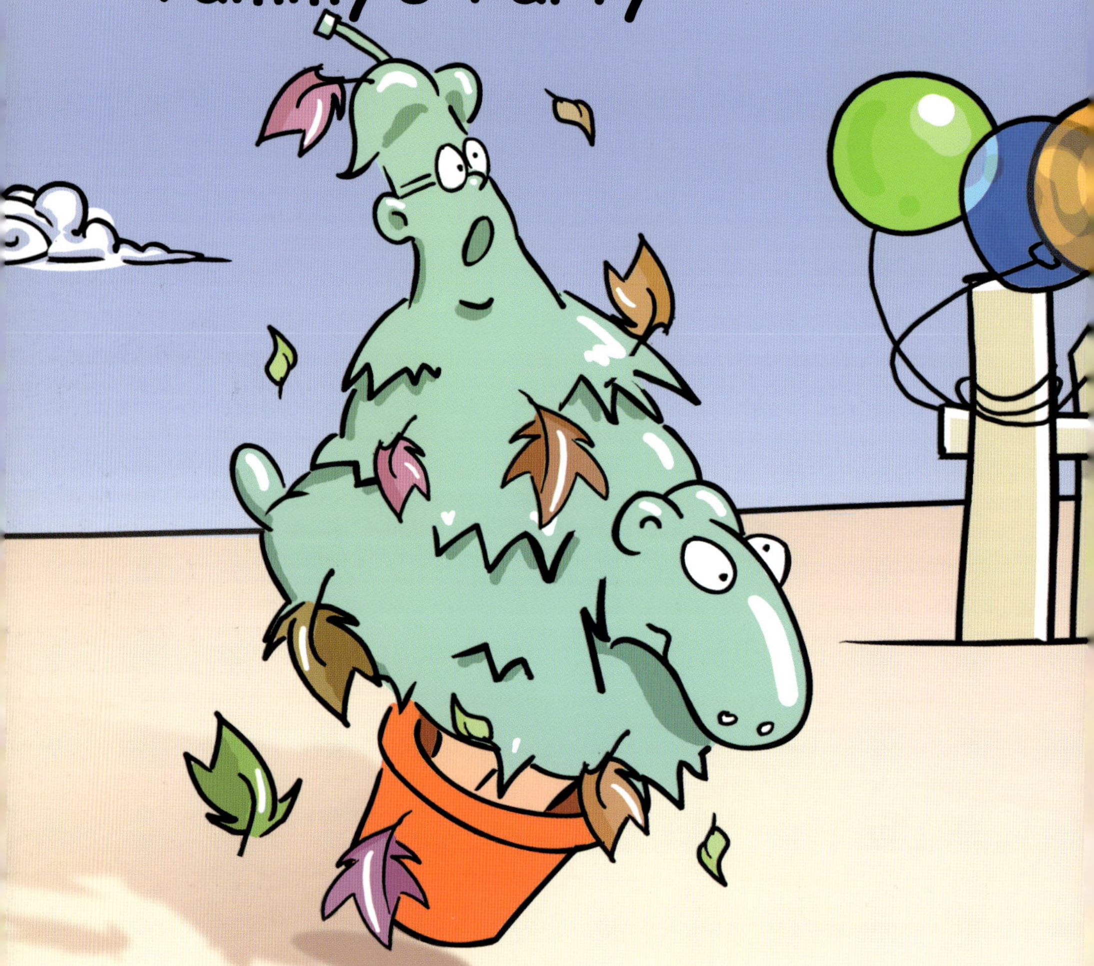

Super Bob hopped down the street. He could see Tammy's house.

It had balloons tied to the front fence.

"Almost there, Otto," Super Bob said with a smile.

"We made it! I think we're in for a treat, Otto. Let's get into it!" Super Bob hopped into Tammy's house. The party was in full swing.

Happy children were laughing and running. Everyone was eating chips, popcorn, and sweets. Then it was time for the piñata.

Super Bob always loved piñatas. He moved in for a closer view.

Little Tammy hit the piñata with a large baseball bat. *Whack!*

"Uh-oh!"

The piñata showered Super Bob with candy.

"Oh, no!" Super Bob laughed. "I'm a decorated tree! And this isn't even a holiday party!"

"You're the funniest birthday cake I've ever seen," said Tammy. The whole party loved Super Bob's big birthday surprise.

Glossary

full swing
everything was happening

gutter
the edge where the road meets the curb

jolt
a sudden jerk

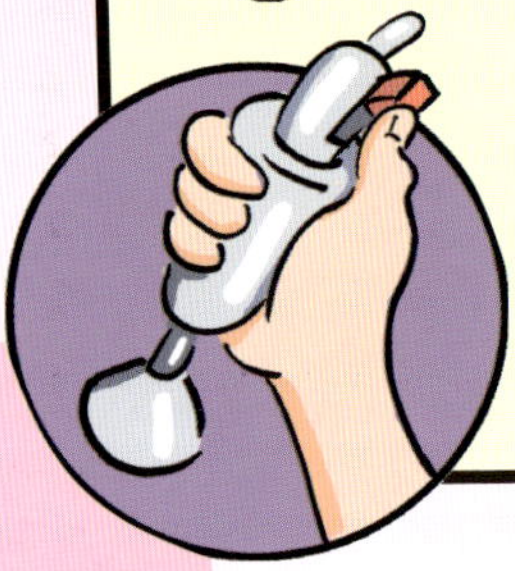

mixer
a machine that mixes things together

piñata
a papier-mâche figure filled with sweets

switch
the control that changes the speed

trusty
can be relied on, dependable

whirlwind
a fast, spinning column of air

Matthew Urmenyhazi

Hidden inside this book is the chocolate key. Can you find it?

One day Matthew bought his two children some chocolates. He put them into his trouser pocket and continued shopping. When he returned to his car, he reached into his pocket and pulled the keys out. The keys were covered in chocolate! He had to lick them clean before starting the car. Passers-by gave him some funny looks!